Decoding Generational Differences:

Fact, fiction ... or
should we just get back to work?

By W. Stanton Smith

Principal

National Director, Next Generation Initiatives

Talent

Deloitte LLP

D1403147

As used in this document, "Deloitte" means Deloitte LLP. Please see www.deloitte.com/us/about
for a detailed description of the legal structure of Deloitte LLP and its subsidiaries.

Decoding Generational Differences: Fact, fiction ... or should we just get back to work?
By W. Stanton Smith

Copyright © 2008 by Deloitte Development LLC.
All rights reserved

No portion of this book may be reproduced in any form, including electronically,
without express permission from Deloitte Development LLC.

Cover design, interior art and layout by Oleonmedia

Contents

Acknowledgements

The talents and experiences of many colleagues have converged with seven years of research and observation to produce this book. I extend my profound thanks to the partners, principals, and directors of Deloitte for providing the resources to complete this important work. Specifically, I'd like to thank the following partners who have been especially supportive along the way: Sharon Allen, Cathy Benko, Barry Salzberg, Jeff Summer, and Jim Wall … and a special thanks to Bill Parrett, who made the request that started it all.

In addition I'd like to thank my Next Generation Initiatives team members, especially Casey Carlson, Gina Martindale, Megan Turk, and Joe Zakierski for their assistance, as well as Lyn Jeffery and Bob Johansen of the Institute for the Future (IFTF) for their wise counsel. Many thanks also to Jackie Boyle for her significant contribution as copyeditor, Dominic Conde of Oleonmedia for his excellent design contributions, and Beth Polazzo of The Polazzo Group for her help in assembling the material. Of course, there are many more that have helped but it is impractical to name them all. You know who you are and I am grateful for the assistance you have provided. Finally, a great big thank you to my wife, Roz. Words are inadequate to express how much her love, support, and good humor mean to me.

Stan Smith
February 2008

Introduction

Want to liven up a leadership meeting? Just introduce the topic of how to deal with the newest generation in the workforce, the millennials.

Some people think that the differences in attitude between this group and more experienced workers are so profound that business, as it is currently conducted, will never be the same again. Others believe that the debate is pointless since the distinctions being made don't constitute real differences. A third group doesn't care if the differences are real or not. They suggest that we all "just get back to work."

So whose view, if any, is closest to reality? That's what we intend to explore in this book.

Why is this topic even worth discussing? Because millennials are fast becoming an influential factor in the workplace … and an increasingly important part of its future.

There are plenty of opinions on the topic, but not a lot of understanding. Discussions of generational differences in the workplace too often produce more heat than light. It is as if we all talk past each other in some kind of code that gets in the way of us really communicating. To promote true communication, we need to decipher that code. Then we'll have a better understanding of what's going on, so we can success-fully move ahead.

At Deloitte, we are actively addressing the topic of genera-tions at work. This book is an outgrowth of this initiative. It is a special edition of the Talent Market Series (TMS), a collec-tion of executive briefings on talent-related topics targeted to Deloitte's partners/principals/directors. This special edition, as with all TMS volumes, is written so that it can be shared with current clients, prospective clients, and other interested parties outside of Deloitte.

This book is designed to:

1. Deepen understanding of millennials, describe how they differ from baby boomers, and explain why you should care.

2. Discuss the solutions Deloitte has developed to ad-dress the business issues arising from generational differences and the changing workforce.

3. Encourage a change in mindset that is necessary if leaders are to be more effective in attracting, retain-ing, and developing millennials as well as others in the workforce.

4. Generate more buy-in and active support for the solu-tions in place and those still to come.

But before we go any further, let me introduce you to our heck-ler. This character represents a "professional skeptic" — the voice of a successful baby boomer who has a bit of an attitude when dealing with generational topics. Our heckler will ask uncomfortable questions (hopefully yours) in a call-out format like the one that follows.

Here we go again with somebody offering another message that's important — even critical — for my future well-being. Of course, I never receive unimportant messages. So ... I'm up to my eyeballs in communications whose content somebody thinks I "have to know" in order to serve my clients, save the polar bears, or whatever. Most promise assorted personal and/or professional epiphanies if I actually read them. So why should I listen to this?

Because I'm a business person with considerable relevant experience on the topic. Even more compelling is that I'm a principal in a major employer of young adults (over 80% of external client–facing employees are under the age of 35). As such, Deloitte has recognized the business relevance of this topic and is already taking steps to address the implications of our research into the related issues.

I am an early baby boomer (another way of saying that I am seasoned) and I came to the topic of generational differences as a true skeptic. If you read on, you'll see the research findings that convinced me that organizations of all shapes and sizes have much to learn if we are to attract and keep the talent we need to succeed. And, by the way, it's not all about the millennials ... it's really about everyone in the workforce.

Our heckler mentions "epiphanies," those moments of blinding insight that occur in the course of ordinary life ... like reading this special edition. Epiphanies are the sole responsibility of the reader.

For my part, I promise research-based conclusions, some examples of solutions to problems, ways to manage dilemmas, and a generally optimistic point of view. And that is: *We all can work together in a very constructive way despite our differences … but only if we keep our minds open and agree to learn from each other as colleagues.*

So skeptics of the world, read on.

> OK, I get the picture. But who invited you to the party and how did you wind up so involved in this generational issue?

Next Generation Initiatives: the origins

In late 2000, I was asked by Jim Wall (then head of Deloitte's Human Resources function), on behalf of Bill Parrett (then Deloitte's chief executive officer), to direct organization-wide reward and recognition programs as well as a research group that created demographic reports to leadership on our employee population. Bill's closing comment to Jim was, "My kids have very different attitudes than I do concerning life, careers … you name it. Something is happening that goes beyond my being old and their being young. And many of our partners are sensing the same thing. Have Stan look into what's behind these changes."

Over the ensuing years, my role as national director of Next Generation Initiatives (NGI) grew into a full-time one. My responsibility was, and is, to study demographic and workforce attitude trends with the purpose of coming up with practical ways to deal with their impact on Deloitte.

NGI grew out of a question about young people's expectations and needs. However, as we did our work, it became apparent that "Next Generation" also referred to the next level of innovative workplace initiatives that were needed — initiatives that affected talent of all generations.

Let's begin with a few definitions that will serve as our standard frame of reference[1]:

Four generations in today's workforce

Veterans — Those born before 1946.

Baby boomers — Those born between 1946 and 1964. They place a heavy emphasis on work and successfully climbing the corporate ladder. Work is an anchor in their lives.

Gen Xers — Those born between 1965 and 1980. They enjoy work, but are more concerned about work-life balance.

Millennials (or Gen Yers) — Those born after 1980. Millennials often have different priorities than their Gen X and baby boomer counterparts. Because of their reliance on technology, they think they can work at any time and anyplace and believe they should be evaluated on work produced — not on how, when, or where they got it done. Curiously, most want long-term relationships with employers, but on their own terms. The real change in workforce attitudes is a decrease in career ambition in favor of more family/personal time and less pressure in life, generally speaking.

From a baby boomer's viewpoint, here's another way of looking at generational differences:

- Baby boomers: "Work, work, work. It's what we're about."

- Gen Xers: "Work. Work more with flexibility. Work even more? Let's talk!"

- Millennials: "Work flexibly anywhere, but I need complete access to information and the answer to 'Why?' Work anytime … on my terms. Work even more? That is so lame. I'm texting all my friends to tell them how lame you are!"

Note: The focus of the book is on baby boomers and millennials, not because Gen X is unimportant, but because the contrast between the boomers and millennials is most striking. Gen Xers, for their part, can play a key role in building and maintaining an effective workplace by acting as a much-needed bridge in communication between the boomers and millennials.

Aren't you just making sweeping generalizations and, as a result, simply indulging in socially acceptable stereotyping?

Research has shown that a generation can be characterized by a certain set of attitudes and beliefs … even if not all in the group share the majority's views. We could look at the world through any number of lenses such as gender, ethnicity, or lifestyle. It's just that we've found that the topic of generational differences provides one of the best frameworks for fostering productive discussions about the changing workforce and workplace.

OK, so now it's time for you to decide whether or not to continue reading … you may be well irritated about the millennials and sick of the topic, but the millennials and their impact on the workforce is a reality that has to be faced.

You need the information in this book to improve your odds of successfully meeting the challenges to come. You need to understand what's really going on in the workplace today and what may well happen over the next few years.

Consider, if you will, the two biggest blind spots of leaders and managers:

1. Not knowing what we don't know.
2. Holding on to those views we believe to be true, but aren't any longer.

"It ain't what you don't know that gets you into trouble. It's what you know for sure that just ain't so."[2]

– Mark Twain

Our promise to you:

- Straightforward answers to our heckler's tough questions.
- Relevant research findings that back up our conclusions.
- Some examples of what can be done.

The role of NGI is not to be some kind of fortune cookie on steroids, but rather to prepare you for what's ahead and provide you with some very effective tools, based on our experiences, to meet the business challenges related to generational differences.

So, what works for the millennials? What works for businesses? And what works for all of us? Read on.

Part I:
What we must decode

Chapter One:
The three dilemmas

In my experience, nothing gets solved without a basic under-standing of where each side stands on an issue. The following are some examples of what I hear.

From the baby boomers:

- This generational stuff is just politically correct rationale that's trying to explain and excuse immature behavior.

- Isn't it catering to and coddling the inexperienced? It's a great example of the inmates running the asylum.

- When is someone going to ask me what I need?

- Doesn't everyone want the same thing anyway?

- This is still planet earth. We already know how to run a successful business. What, if anything, can we learn from these kids that's really new?

- Can we go back to work now? These kids will either get with the program or they'll leave.

At the same time, I hear comments like these from the young-est members of the workforce:

- I don't get it … my managers are barely technologically literate, yet they're never open to suggestions on how to improve a process with technology. What's up with this attitude?

- Don't they want to go home at night? They act as if I should want to work 60 to 70 hours a week, year in and year out … I'm not afraid of hard work, but that's not the only thing I want to do with my life.

- Boomers tell me, "I'm older, have more experience, and stop asking so many questions." I want to tell them, "That's right, you are older … older than dirt and you don't answer my questions either because you don't know the answer or you wish you'd asked the same questions when you were my age and didn't have the nerve."

What do these statements have in common?

- They reveal attitudes that don't work toward the common good.

- They demonstrate the need to understand what's behind our viewpoints and how much we have to learn to leverage our strengths and to understand where and why we may differ.

> Aren't these statements just attributable to the age-old differences between those with real-life experience and those without?

On the surface, this may appear to be true … but our research and experience indicate a much more complex set of dilemmas that require decoding.

A dilemma offers multiple viable options, none of which alone or together will provide a lasting solution. Dilemmas have to be managed or resolved continuously. Owing to their complexity, dilemmas may require apparently contradictory actions to be successfully managed.[1]

Through research and observation, we have uncovered three major dilemmas or realities that we must accept if we are to understand what is going on in the workplace and then be able to do something about it.

These are:

- Formative years dilemma: The conditions that produced us (baby boomers and some early Gen Xers), and enabled us to become professionals, are largely gone and can't be replicated.
  - But at the same time, we are finding it difficult to imagine how else to develop our younger employees and still run our business profitably.
- Readiness dilemma: There are gaps in the readiness of millennials to enter the workforce that we, as employers, must help close.
  - But at the same time, there is the near-term prospect of significantly fewer millennials ready for knowledge-based jobs.
- Experienced talent dilemma: There is a ready and sufficient supply of experienced workers aged 45 and older in the population.
  - But at the same time, leveraging this supply of experienced workers requires rethinking of how we

do work. This change is uncomfortable since we're not sure exactly how to do it.

Formative years dilemma

Baby boomers and some early Gen Xers grew up in a world with the following characteristics:

- An educational system that, relative to today, appears to have emphasized a higher level of proficiency in basic literacy tools such as spelling, grammar, and written expression.

- A greater sense of personal security. For example, children had a much less formally scheduled life outside school hours. They could, for the most part, be safely sent out into the neighborhood to play, make new friends, and fend for themselves.

- Considerably less connectivity through technology. There was little else besides the radio, television, and telephone, and this technology was far less intrusive than today's technology.

- The high likelihood of a stay-at-home mother who took care of the domestic side of life.

- More relaxed expectations of turnaround time on requests in business, comparatively speaking.

- Face-to-face contact as the norm, since people had to go to an office to work. There was no other realistic way to accomplish day-to-day business.

- Less consumerism. There were fewer products, services, and/or experiences to buy … and comparatively less money to spend.

The list goes on, but the point is that baby boomers and early Gen Xers have reacted to the world in a rational way based on the conditions they encountered.

The newest generation in the workplace, the millennials, is also reacting rationally to the conditions in which they grew up.

Some of their realities are:

- An educational system that apparently does not emphasize basic tools in the same way it did when baby boomers and early Gen Xers were in school.
- A far more scheduled childhood and one that seems more threatening both at school and in the neighborhood.
- Infinitely more connectivity to the greater world through technology, combined with a belief that electronic or digital connections with other people are as acceptable as face-to-face communication.
- Greatly increased expectations of much quicker turnaround of requests in both business and personal life.
- Due to technology, a strong belief that work can be done any time, anyplace and that people are connected 24/7.
- A vastly increased array of products, services, and experiences; very high brand awareness and expectation on the part of consumers to interact with anything that they consume.

This list also could go on, but the point is that both sides need to recognize that different experiences breed different ways of making sense of the world.

Readiness dilemma

Businesses today are using considerable resources preparing new employees to do the most basic work. Case in point: the number of remedial writing courses that even high-profile corporations must provide to get their "high-talent graduates" up to speed in writing for business. Professors tell me that they spend so much time helping young people write properly and read with comprehension that they are unable to cover the same amount of technical material that they once did during a particular course.

Furthermore, many of these millennials object to being sub-jected to the pressure of "even more work." A true story from a highly selective college illustrates the point: Late in the semester, a history professor assigned a major project that needed to be completed and turned in during the two weeks prior to finals. One of the most gifted students approached the professor and said, "You have assigned this difficult project at the end of the semester with no regard to the rest of our academic workload and extracurricular activities. This puts us under unnecessary pressure and obviously proves that you have no regard for any other part of our lives. So, I'm not go-ing to do this project." The astonished professor reminded the student that he currently had an A in the course and would at best receive a C if he failed to complete the project. The stu-dent responded that he was aware of the impact on his grade and was willing to accept it. He said, "College is a ticket to be punched. My future success is not meaningfully correlated with my grade point average."[2]

I think you'll agree that this story represents, among other things, the existence of a rather large gap in understanding about how the world operates. With regard to the story, it is interesting to note that several other students joined the boycott for the same reasons expressed by their fellow student. The implication is that even the best are coming to us with gaps that must be filled. A further implication is that we will be devoting more resources than we have in the past to bring this generation up to speed during their first few years in the business world.

At the same time, there will be fewer talented people available in the workplace. Research on the current U.S. high-school population provides a glimpse of just how tight the labor market could become if we don't begin now to create more interest in careers related to our business.

Fact: There are currently about 16.5 million students in grades 9 through 12. It is estimated that only 33% will graduate from high school, enroll in college right away, and graduate with at least a bachelor's degree within 4 to 6 years. That results in about 5.4 million college graduates potentially coming into the labor pool over the four-year period from 2011 to 2014.[3]

At this point we draw upon research done on behalf of Deloitte by Weekly Reader Research (WRR).[4] The findings reported the career preferences of 12- to 18-year-olds in the U.S. based on a list of 45 typical careers. Approximately 2.3% indicated interest in accounting and business consulting if they were starting a career today. If we apply the 2.3% factor to the projected number of college graduates (5.4 million), we get a pool of 124,200 for the entire period, or about 31,000 entering the workforce annually seeking jobs in accounting and business consulting. This number compares to an estimated 54,000 accounting graduates (bachelor's and master's degrees) per year currently entering the market, and would constitute a nearly 43% drop in supply in accounting graduates alone. Note that we've excluded from this analysis other degrees from which we might recruit for business consultants.

Implication: This admittedly rough estimate illustrates that competition in the talent marketplace will be even more fierce than it is today. Currently, the Big Four professional services organizations hire between 20,000 and 25,000 students directly out of college annually. Deloitte hires about 5,400, including interns, across all our businesses. What's more, the competition is intensified by the fact that we must hire from a limited number of academic majors, given the technical nature of our businesses. Clearly, we face the high probability of an exceptionally tight labor pool.

> Sounds plausible, but this has to be a worst case scenario. I've seen AICPA data showing that the number of accounting graduates continues to climb. Who's telling the truth?

The most recent American Institute of Certified Public Accountants (AICPA) supply/demand report (2005)[5] shows accounting enrollments and graduates up 19% from 2000 to 2004, but enrollments in accounting majors up only 1.5% from 2003 through 2004 (the most recent year reported). This latter statistic suggests that enrollments may well be leveling off. Even at the current enrollment and graduation levels, the market for talent is difficult. Just imagine how much more challenging it will be if the underlying supply of relevant talent for us diminishes at all. The point is that there is a high likelihood that the inflow into accounting majors, to say nothing of the other degree backgrounds that we seek, will not increase from 2011 to 2014. As a result, supply will tighten further.

Experienced talent dilemma

The American professional workforce will continue to age and shrink in the next decade. The median age of the overall population and the labor force will increase as the majority of the baby boomer generation (born between 1946 and 1964) moves into their 50s/60s and the oldest, into their 70s over the next 10 years. According to the U.S. Census for the year 2000, 20% of the population was 55 or older; by 2015, that segment will grow to 28%. In addition, from now until 2015, workers aged 55 to 64 will be the fastest growing segment of the labor force.

By the end of this year (2008), it is estimated that over the previous five-year period about 24 million baby boomer workers will have left the active workforce, primarily from executive, administrative, and managerial jobs. Gen X presents a much smaller pool of available workers, and will not be able to fill the positions left vacant by retirements. The pool of available workers among those aged 25 to 44 will have decreased by 7% from the level five years previous (2003), resulting in a significant labor shortage. In fact, every year for the next 30 years, there will be fewer young people to replace retiring workers (assuming retirements continue at historical rates). The labor shortages will continue well into the future, as average annual growth of the workforce is projected to hover at around 1% through 2015.[6]

This dilemma further impacts the supply problems of accounting and tax graduates, as many of the faculty teaching in these two areas will retire or be eligible to retire over the next 5 to 10 years. Consequently, the demand for those with the relevant doctoral degrees will far outstrip supply. Resolution of this supply/demand imbalance will take a consistent long-term effort to resolve. The Deloitte Foundation has implemented initiatives designed to address this issue in conjunction with interested parties in the accounting profession and academia.

The 3 divides

As if these dilemmas weren't enough, certain realities have fundamentally affected how millennials view the world, including three critical ones that, for the sake of discussion, we'll call the 3 divides.

- Technology.
- Attitude toward business.
- Consumer attitude mindset.

The intensity and extent of exposure to technology has had a major impact on how people perceive work as well as when, where, and how it can be done. It permits a 24/7 connection to others, but especially to work. As such, this 24/7 connectivity removes the traditional constraints of office hours and location. Technology encourages networks and a lack of boundaries that makes operating in hierarchies problematic and challenges traditional ways of doing and managing work. At first, this difference appears to be generational, but it is not. It is the difference between those who view technology as a tool or a toy and those who see it as the way they interact with the world — an extension of themselves or, as it has been said, their oxygen.

The next important factor is the view that millennials (as well as their parents and teachers) have about business values. They believe that despite what corporations say, businesses value financial success far more than they value the people that work for them or the communities in which they live.[7] This view appears to be based on the negative impacts of mergers, acquisitions, and other business trends. This skepticism about business can be summarized by this comment made by a college student who was strongly supported by others in her focus group and in subsequent ones: "We are looking to be loyal to an employer if that employer will be loyal to us, but we don't think business operates that way today."

The third potent divide is that of consumer attitude. Millennials, as we've noted, have been raised to be consumers … to question value … to demand and expect high-quality, easy-to-handle "microwavable experiences." This is the world in which they were raised; thus it's understandable that they carry these expectations with them as they consume everything — including careers.

How's this for an example: On the first day of class, a university accounting professor asked all of her students to state their name, hometown, and what they hoped to get out of the class. The students completed their introductions and then there was an awkward moment of silence as they stared at her. So she asked, "Is there a problem? What do you want?"

A student answered, "We would like to know why you believe that you're qualified to teach us." The professor was aghast, but answered the question. Later, she asked me why they would even ask the question. My answer was that this is an example of the millennials demanding value … they are asking the question, "After 25 years of teaching, are you still in the game, still excited about what you do?" Paraphrasing what more than one millennial has said to me, "We're aware of how much it costs to get a degree … so we want to know that we're getting value for our parents' investment."[8]

Here's another example of how millennials believe that they have power as consumers and are willing to assert that power. The experienced varsity coach of a college swimming and diving team resigned unexpectedly at the beginning of the season. The college administration hired an individual with coaching experience (none in swimming, however) on a temporary basis to get through the season. After a few weeks, one of the better swimmers quit the team. He told the coach, "You don't know much of anything about swimming, and therefore I can't learn much from you. If both the team and I continue to perform well, there is a good possibility that you will be hired full-time. If that happens, I will miss my senior year of swimming because I won't return to swim if you are the coach." By the end of the season, others had complained and the team results were below expectations. The outcome? You guessed it — the coach's contract was not renewed and a coach with swimming experience was hired.[9]

Now put aside your questions about the level of maturity exhibited and the possibility that there's more to the story than appears here. The point is the consumer mindset — the level of sophistication shown in an understanding of how the world works and in the perception that as consumers these young people believe they have rights to exercise. So it should be no surprise, then, that they will likely behave as engaged consumers in the workplace.

Chapter Two:
The 3 R's and 3 C's

There is good news and bad news. The good news is that all generations basically want and value the same things. The bad news is that priorities, expectations, and behaviors may differ noticeably. People may want the same things, but they want them delivered in different packages, depending on when and how they grew up. Let's take the millennials as an example:

- Changes in family structure have affected their focus on work and desire for increased flexibility in work schedules, work setting, job design, and career planning.

- They were raised to be consumers — they're even called "engaged consumers" by marketers. These young people want to interact with and influence anything that they consume, including careers.

- We raised them to question authority and demand value for money.

- They grew up as "technology natives," a fact that profoundly affects what they expect from life and how they relate to it.

- They came of age in a world of layoffs and corporate scandals, fostering the belief that businesses in general, and big businesses in particular, value their own financial gain far above all else, and that business talk about the importance of people is largely insincere.

In contrast, baby boomers were brought up in a very different world; consequently their experiences shape their beliefs and desires differently from their millennial counterparts.

So what are the 3 R's and 3 C's?[1] People want to be:

- **Respected**
  - To have interesting and meaningful work to do and to enjoy it in the process.
  - To have the opportunity to learn, grow, and improve one's prospects in life.
  - To work and live in positive/friendly environments, free from prejudice and favoritism.
  - To have some flexibility in schedules and some control over one's life.
  - To be trusted and to be able to trust one's leaders.
  - To be loyal and have that loyalty returned in equal measure.

- **Recognized** for accomplishments (both monetarily and non-monetarily).

- **Remembered** as having made a difference and associated with businesses that care about their people, community, and environment.

- **Coached** rather than subjected to fault-finding.

- **Consulted** on actions that will affect them.

- **Connected** to their employer and its mission (to understand the mission and where and how they fit into it, and to feel a meaningful part of the whole … personally as well as professionally).

> OK, so everyone wants to be treated "nice."
> When are you going to give me some real
> meat on how to deal with these millennials?

Fair enough … let's decode the mysteries of dealing with the millennials when it comes to the 3 R's and 3 C's. Keep in mind that millennials:

- Respond poorly to those who act in an authoritarian manner and/or who expect to be respected due to higher rank alone.

- Believe they can learn quickly, take on significant responsibility, and make major contributions far sooner than baby boomers think they can.

- Have been raised to feel valuable and very positive about themselves; they consider it a sign of disrespect to be expected to do things just because "this is the way it has always been done" or "you have to pay your dues."

- See repetitive tasks as a poor use of their energy and time … and see it as an example of how they are not being respected/taken seriously or are being subjected to an old-school mentality.

- Respond poorly to inflexible, hierarchical organizations and respond best to more networked, less hierarchical situations.

- Expect flexible schedules. ("The technology permits it, so why not? Evaluate me on output, not input — on the work product itself, not where or when or how I do the work.")

- Do not want to be taken advantage of. They do not have sufficient trust in businesses to believe that these organizations will really make good on the promise of lots of money someday in the distant future if they consistently perform well over their career.

Decoding how to manage millennials so everyone benefits

- Adopt a mindset of thinking flexibly.

- Realize that they want to work with friends (colleagues with complementary skills who are simpatico).

- Show them that you respect what they bring to the party (they see their lack of experience as bringing a new perspective that is needed in the business world).

- Let them have fun (millennials will work hard, but "hey dude, chill out, we're not saving the world from alien invaders").

- Don't take it all so seriously; a sense of humor is a handy quality to have.

- Challenge and stretch their minds with a variety of assignments.

- Lead as an experienced colleague helping them to

avoid mistakes and become professionals, not as a know-it-all boss.

- Be a mentor (millennials seem more trusting of senior leaders than baby boomers and Gen Xers were, and they are very willing to be mentored).

Now for some examples of how to manage millennials:

- Provide engaging experiences that develop transferable skills. By making them more employable, we actually increase the odds that they will stay.

- Provide a rationale for the work you've asked them to do and the value it adds.

- Provide variety.

- Grow teams and networks with great care … develop the tools and processes to support faster response and more innovative solutions.

- Explicitly reward extra effort and excellence of results.

- Pay close attention to helping them navigate work and family issues.

- Demonstrate a willingness and availability to talk through their perceived problems, i.e., just listen.

Playing nice in the sandbox: what millennials expect from management communication

They want it to be:

- Positive.
- Respectful.
- Motivational.

- Electronic.

- In person, if the message is really important.

- Timely.

Who knew it could be so complicated? Decoding the favorite learning styles of millennials

They want learning that is:

- In networks, teams, or swarms (leaderless groups that are linked by the use of technology; an example is the use of text messaging by teens at a mall).

- Multimedia.

- Engaging and stimulating.

- Experiential. (Business simulations are becoming the next wave in games and they actually help familiarize young people with a business previously unknown to them. Simulations also offer the opportunity to track skill development and open a new source of talent tracking and recruitment.)

Now for a quick Q&A session with our heckler

> I wanted what these young people want when I was their age but I had to adapt to business realities. Won't the same thing happen to them?

Certainly, to an extent. But two things are very different today compared to when the baby boomers entered the workforce 30+ years ago or the Gen Xers some 15 to 20 years ago:

1. Demographics and the law of supply and demand are at work. That is, there are now far fewer millennials than there were baby boomers at the time of initial entry into the workplace; therefore, the probability of millennials getting a lot more of what they want is much higher than it was for previous generations.

2. Technology exists to support millennials' preference to work more flexibly and virtually; this capacity to work anyplace and at any time simply did not exist until very recently.

> What, if anything, can we learn from these young people?

The millennials are coming into the workforce with networking and global-mindedness skills from which older generations can learn. In addition, millennials are technology natives who can drive a role reversal by mentoring technology-challenged baby boomers. And finally, maybe we can learn something useful from the millennials (and Gen Xers), who work more flexibly and who have a more dual-centric focus on both work and family.

> Why should a business leader care what young people think, especially those not even out of high school or middle school? They're inexperienced and will change their minds anyway.

It is true that young people often change their minds. However, our research shows that during these formative teen years, they are making major decisions as to which college to attend and what to major in. They are forming opinions that will influence them for a lifetime. This attitude makes their negative views about large businesses especially troublesome. Why? Because it is likely that if and when these young people do join big business, their skepticism may present a significant challenge as they adapt to their new working environment.

> The attitudes of these millennials just reflect a stage in life; they'll outgrow their current views. In any event, once they have family obligations, they'll change their attitudes, won't they?

While people generally become more conservative as they age, research shows that core generational values change very little. For example, both Gen Xers and millennials are very family-oriented; therefore, it is unlikely that they'll become significantly less family focused. Such focus is a defining difference between these generations and the baby boomers.

> We'll just have to work harder at finding those young people who will do it our way, won't we?

This tactic may meet with some success, but likely will fall far short in achieving the needed numbers, given the demographics and workforce attitudes discussed in this book.

The generational differences
are exaggerated anyway, right?

Possibly, but research and our experience indicate that the differences are real and mainstream; they are not confined to just a tiny number in each generation.

Isn't what motivated me in my 20s the
same as what motivates young people today?

There will be instances when this is true, but on balance it is risky to make that assumption. The documented effects of growing up with technology and the attitudes and expectations of Gen Xers and millennials are in themselves enough to make us question the validity of the assumption behind this question.

Chapter Three: The great technology divide

Millennials grew up with computers and cell phones the way baby boomers and Gen Xers grew up with typewriters and corded telephones. Remember when party lines were really party lines? The implications of this technological disparity are profound: Baby boomers see technology as a tool, or even a toy, while younger workers see it as an extension of themselves. These millennials see themselves as "technology natives," moderate multitaskers who get a lot done. Most of them mix entertainment and work.

> Mixing entertainment and work ... that's just a politically correct way of saying they are goofing off at the expense of the business. How can these kids justify playing video games at work?

First of all, there is a real difference in perception. As more than one millennial has said to me, "Who are you kidding; we're on call 24/7 … why don't you admit it?"

Remember when no one called you at home unless there was

an impending disaster? Remember how when you went home, you went home? You were, in effect, disconnected from work.

Not anymore. With round-the-clock e-mails and demands for answers, knowledge workers no longer make much of a distinction between working and non-working hours. Consequently, millennials believe that they need to take breaks throughout the day. In earlier times, we may have walked around the office or turned on the radio … they may turn to games or use their iPods or view YouTube.

> *How in the world can sitting in front of a computer and playing for even a few minutes NOT hurt a business?*

An excellent source for understanding the impact of video games on young people is the book *The Kids Are Alright: How the Gamer Generation Is Changing the Workplace,* by John C. Beck and Mitchell Wade. In it the authors describe seven habits of typical "gamers" (typically millennials and Gen Xers, though some baby boomers are gamers as well), adapted here for our purposes[1]:

1. **Everyone can succeed.** Gamers grew up in a world where literally everyone can succeed at just about anything. By working hard enough (and long enough), it is possible for every player to win these games … the trick is to keep the game interesting, challenging, and fun.

2. **You gotta play the odds.** Millennials grew up playing games of chance. A probability algorithm has been built

into almost every game they've played. A survey conducted by Beck and Wade found that gamers are twice as likely as boomers to believe success in life is due to luck. This prepares them to shrug off pretty serious setbacks (remember the dot-com bust?) as learning experiences in which their luck just ran out. It also teaches them to analyze the game they are playing and, if the odds don't seem good, to look elsewhere. Of course, there are times in life, like falling in love or choosing a career, when the odds aren't what's important. A little coaching (by us "old timers") could help here.

3. **Learn from the team.** Gamers are surprisingly good at teamwork. They love working together and help-ing each other. They often play games in groups. Even the youngest are encouraged to learn new skills, since the game stays more interesting when everyone in the room has competitive abilities.

   However, in the world of video games, there is usually no adult present. Gamers don't practice before they play video games; they learn by doing … and doing it togeth-er. So, whenever you can, resist the urge to give an order — often you'll teach better and get a better result by playing the role of a senior colleague who is introducing a group of gamers to a problem that we can solve together … then let them have at it.

4. **Trust strategy guides, not the bosses.** In video games, the Level Boss is the hardest obstacle to get past to achieve your goal. So gamers can have issues with traditional authority. What they love, though, are strat-egy guides — those books, blogs, etc. — written from

a peer's perspective, with inside info on how to win. (In many games, it's just about impossible to win without these cheat codes.) So, want to share hard-won knowledge? Position yourself as a fellow player who has been there and can offer some strategy tips, not as a boss.

5. **Watch the map.** Video games are complex — just watch one for a while. But they're a lot more transparent than the world we know. One feature gamers count on is the overhead meta map that shows where they are in relation to other players, goals, obstacles, and resources. Young people from this generation function best if they know exactly where they are, what they need to win, and who's ahead of (or behind) them. They need a map, a guide, and some external metrics to show how far they have to go and what's in their way. As you may have noticed, real life seldom provides all that. But you may be able to teach them how to develop their own meta maps … or at least learn how to operate without one.

6. **Can't see it? Ignore it.** For gamers, the action — and there's plenty of that — is all on the surface. In a game, there are almost never truly unseen enemies. That's quite a contrast to human organizations, whether they are families, companies, or communities, where you may be weakened or frustrated by decisions from people you can't confront. Gamers can become confused, baffled, and even furious when thwarted by unseen forces in organizations. Of course, you can't make your gamers' world transparent. But you can make some processes clearer, and head off some nasty surprises.

7. **Demand the right team.** In gaming, there's nothing more frustrating than playing with someone who doesn't get it. That's why multiplayer games offer certain regions where "newbies" practice their skills before they foist themselves on others, and why designers create mechanisms for people who just shouldn't be in a high-level area to go to a less competitive island, world, or other area of the game. Good gamers will flee places where there aren't enough high-quality players. They do the same thing in other parts of their life as well. Groups thrown together by luck, tradition, or a desire for balance just don't work for them. Help the gamers you care about find teams that match their level — and their passion for a particular challenge — and you'll be amazed at what they can do.

Are you beginning to see how you can make millennials' habits work for you and for the business? All it takes is the genuine desire to learn from each other.

> If these kids have their attention on games and other forms of technology, how can they be working effectively and how can it pay off for us?

Deloitte conducted a series of studies on young people (generally aged 14 to 21).[2] These studies were done in conjunction with the Institute for the Future and focused on the effect of technology on study and work habits as well as their expectations of employers. Here are some implications for business leaders:

- Avoid preconceived notions of attention span and media use when assessing youth work practices. Don't assume that because young people work with lots of media and technology "open" at any given time, they are less focused. Assess the results. However, messages that are initiated by others versus media controlled by oneself may be as much a distraction for younger people as they are for older workers.

- Look to entry-level talent as a source of new learning and knowledge-management practices. Few senior people have the time to keep up with the rapid changes in communications technology. In the next decade, entry-level workers will be bringing a host of new knowledge-management practices they have forged through years of experience. Reverse mentoring is one way to make sure that we as business leaders have our figurative fingers on the pulse of what is possible.

- Build a teen-friendly online presence. Since teens are oriented toward the Internet for learning and playing, businesses should develop a clear online strategy to attract talented kids and nurture the future workforce. Deloitte is already doing this; these projects will be discussed later in the book.

- Provide flexibility around media choice. Understanding that many young people develop their work habits with a broad attention range means employers will need to provide these talented workers with a host of tools and choices. If employers don't provide them, the young people are likely to modify their tools themselves.

- Provide clear standards for professional communication. We don't yet understand the long-term impact of a formative media experience and work style that mixes formal and informal communication styles. Will the casual style characteristic of e-mail, instant messaging, and texting creep into more formal presentations in the workplace, for example? One way to explore this would be to survey managers who work with entry-level employees. Are they seeing any difference in communication styles, or lack of skills, in particular communication areas, and are these differences negatively impacting client or customer service?

> So you're saying that we shouldn't worry about the short attention spans that we see in young people?

Not at all. I am emphasizing the need to accept the fact that there are some positives that can come out of the effect that technology is having on young people. Businesses still have to assure themselves that all the work done with "continuous partial attention" is of the quality that is demanded by the marketplace.

> *I believe we overdo this technology thing. These kids come to me with technology solutions to problems I didn't know I had. I can't assess the viability of these ideas anyway and besides, we seem to be doing quite well with the "solutions" we currently use.*

Remember that we as leaders are experiencing a phenomenon that just might be new to humans … that the older we are the less we know about a major force in our world — technology. In contrast, the younger you are the more you know about technology. That's why reverse mentoring makes sense, so leaders can at least become aware of what they don't know and at best have help in evaluating these technology proposals.

Also recall that millennials have differing views about technology because of their early and continuous exposure to it. A typical perspective is expressed in the following excerpt from an e-mail I received: "We've discussed how people my age grew up with email, internet, instant messaging, etc, but for someone my age (early 20s in a first job out of college), it's almost inconceivable to think about what it was like before those things existed. For example, I cannot imagine how essays were written before word processors. It seems unbearable. In a general sense, it astounds me that business was ever carried out before all these tools existed."[3]

Experienced types may well smile at this "beginner's" perspective. However, I urge you to consider the profound implications of how differently work and the workplace are viewed by millennials today as a consequence of technological change. Just compare today's environment to the business environment with much less sophisticated technology that existed some 20+ years ago, when most of today's leaders were "beginners" themselves in the work world.

> What's up with gender or diversity differences that are supposed to be everywhere? Why haven't you said anything about those issues?

Interestingly, there are no material differences in attitude based on gender or other diversity measures when it comes to technology.[2,4] This is not to say that there are no differences between teenaged boys and girls in the use of technology. However, the research indicates that these differences are much less evident as both males and females join the post-college, full-time workforce.

Chapter Four:
Attitudes toward big business

> Does it really matter what young people think about business in high school or even earlier?

The quick answer: No doubt that it does matter. Millennials will soon be the majority of our employees ... the talent we will rely on.

In this chapter we'll decode the attitudes of millennials toward big business by analyzing the findings of a major study performed on behalf of Deloitte by WRR in 2007.[1] According to this report, "... the good news is that America's 39 million middle- and high-school students — no matter what their age, gender, or racial differences — generally have a positive attitude toward work and careers."

The following points are the most important to keep in mind when considering the attitudes of young people (aged 12 to 18, in this case) toward work and careers:

- 79% think that having a job/profession they really like is an important part of having a happy life.

- 70% believe that liking what they do is more important to them than making lots of money.
- 65% want to climb the corporate ladder to a point and then have the flexibility to get on and off it as their life needs change.

Yet, they're conflicted about the value of climbing the corporate ladder:

- 59% agreed with the statement "to climb the corporate ladder is well worth it."
- 47% agreed with the statement "to climb the corporate ladder requires too much sacrifice."
- 53% believe that "people put too much emphasis on work and professions."
- 38% agreed with the statement "making a lot of money is more important to me than anything else."

So, what do these apparent contradictions mean? It seems as if young people want a job that they love, but they are not willing to do just anything for the money … and they're not so sure about the value of climbing that corporate ladder.

Now, take what you've just learned and look at the following attitudes that young people have toward big business:

- 79% agreed with the fact that "a good company continually invests in its employees."
- 78% believed that "a good company continually invests in its community."
- 77% believed that "a good company thinks about its impact on the environment."

Just what do these kids want?

Well, they want to work for the good company. That's for sure. And, according to America's youth, the good company is one that has achieved balance across all three areas (employees, community, and environment).

- 69.5% agreed that "big business is always talking about how they care about people — their employees, customers, and communities — but they would put money and profits in front of all of these if it came down to it." (13.4% disagreed with the statement and 16.2% selected "I just don't know.")

- 41.4% agreed that "business usually considers the non-financial, i.e., people, impact of their decisions." (33.7% disagreed with the statement while 23.5% selected "I just don't know.")

- 34.4% agreed with the statement "all that business should care about is making the greatest profit for its owners." (51.0% disagreed and 14.1% selected "I just don't know.")

Those responding "I just don't know" adopt a "wait and see" attitude, meaning they would make a decision on a case-by-case basis. If you assume a 50/50 split of those selecting "I just don't know" and then incorporate the split into the results above, the results are even more dramatic: (1) the proportion agreeing with the view that businesses are essentially driven by profit rises to about three-fourths; (2) nearly half would disagree that businesses consider non-financial impacts on people; and (3) nearly 6 out of 10 would disagree that business should only be focused on profit. The point is that the views of these young people really are out of sync with the way business is conducted in our economy today in the U.S.

Why are their beliefs so out of sync? Based on our focus groups and other discussions with young people, it is reasonable to conclude that what they observed and experienced growing up in a world of cutbacks, asset plays, and corporate scandals has had a significant impact on their views.

Millennials think that big business has allowed its values to become misaligned, and it is this balance and alignment of values that define the good company. Remember, they want to work for the good company … the one that cares about its employees, the community, and the environment. This good company is as much about how work is done (fun and engaging, never boring, anywhere, at any time) as it is about the actual work product.

Take a look at the following chart that measures what "should be/is" the reality with respect to caring about clients, making a profit, and caring about employees and community concerns. Note that the young respondents believe equal attention should be paid to making money and making employees happy. Interestingly, they also put pleasing customers as the most important objective of a business. In contrast, they believe businesses are primarily profit driven, with other stakeholders far behind in relative importance.

Stakeholder Orientation

Orientation	Weight SHOULD have	Weight DOES have
Customer orientation — making the greatest products and services and keeping the customer happy	36	18
Financial orientation — making the greatest profit and keeping owners happy	25	58
Employee orientation — being a great place to work and keeping employees happy	25	14
Community orientation — making the towns and cities in which they are located the best they can be and keeping their neighbors happy	14	10

Source: Deloitte/Weekly Reader Research: *Accounting and the Next Generation of Workers,*
February 2007 (see references section)

The level of disparity between their beliefs and their perception of what's happening has heavily influenced how millennials view life and in particular their business life.

In addition, our research shows that:

- They prefer to stay with one employer.
- They prefer to work in a small organization.
- They highly value honesty and respect from senior executives.

Decode please ... aren't we just talking about kids who'll grow up and realize how things have to get done in the world? What am I missing?

What you may be missing is the profound impact that two divides — technology and attitudes toward business — have on these young people. Consider the following key findings from the 2007 WRR study:

- Caring is as important as pay, benefits, and opportunities for advancement when young people evaluate career opportunities and employers. Survey respondents want to work for a firm that cares … about them as employees, and about the community and environment in which they operate.

- Careers need to be interesting and fun. There is very low tolerance for boredom.

- Young people pass through four well-defined stages in career decision-making: contemplation (ages 10 to 11), diversification (ages 12 to 14), canalization (ages 15 to 16), and activation (ages 17 to 18). It is interesting to note that by 10 years of age, many young people are seriously considering different career alternatives.

- Each stage is characterized by changes in the size of the consideration set: the number of careers of interest and the information sources relied on and used for gathering information about all the (often contradictory) careers in the consideration set. The bottom line here is that young people are most open to the widest set of career possibilities between the ages of 12 and 14. Thereafter, they begin to narrow the set of careers under consideration.

- In general, America's young people are interested in what is going on in the world of business and believe kids should start learning about business, finance, money, and investments in the 4th grade.

What this means is that young people are overwhelmingly skeptical about business rhetoric such as how much business cares about people. This generation also believes that business does not meaningfully consider the impact of its decisions on people, and finally, very few of them believe that business should have profit as its main preoccupation.

Our study also found something else — that there is another constituency that is very influential, and one that you need to consider: parents and teachers. Their views about business are even more skeptical than those of their children or students.

That means that in order to attract the best and brightest, we need to start getting our message out to people who we might never have considered vital to the future of a business … those parents and teachers.

It's something so important that we've started a number of programs that we'll discuss in more detail in a later chapter.

Chapter Five:
The consumer mindset

> *Why do these millennials approach life as "engaged consumers"? Isn't this just a fancy way of saying that they want to be catered to and avoid working hard for the results they expect?*

There may be some naïveté in this consumer approach to life, but we are where we are with regard to this consumer mentality. So how can we better cope with this mentality and even leverage it to our mutual benefit?

Let's begin with one of the more profound mega-facts[1]: The family structure in the U.S. continues to evolve and it is strikingly different from when baby boomers were children during the 1950s and 1960s, and when most of them first started business careers in the 1970s. These changes have had a significant impact on the attitudes of workers, particularly those who are under the age of 40.

Nobody at home

Fact: Male heads of household, i.e., a husband who is the sole breadwinner for the household while the wife stays home, constituted 56% of employees in 1950, according to the census that year. The 2000 census showed that the percentage of male heads of household fell to 21% of employees. Most married women are now employed — an increase from 37% in 1967 to 61% in 2000.

Implication: Most of our talent has no stay-at-home partner to handle personal matters while they are at work. Our people must divide their energy and focus between work and home.

Dual incomes create options

Fact: Over the past 30 years, women have gained access to a wider range of better-paying jobs. In 55% of U.S. families, women now earn more than half the household's income.

Implication: Employers no longer have as much leverage as they previously had over workers. At least for the duration of a reasonable-length job search, one partner in a two-income family can feasibly quit an unsatisfying job with manageable financial consequences. This option is less available to individuals who are the sole support for a household.

Single-minded focus on work is declining

Fact: Almost 90% of Gen X and millennial workers and more than 75% of baby boomers have either a primary focus on family, or they divide their focus between work and family. Gen X fathers spend 3.4 hours per day with their children compared to an average of 2.2 hours that baby boomer fathers spent with their equivalent-age children 25 years ago. Children in two-parent families are actually receiving more combined attention from their parents today than they did 25 years ago.

Implication: Many business leaders have a stay-at-home partner and a single-minded focus on work. This stands in stark
contrast to the small proportion of today's younger workforce
with a stay-at-home partner and a primary focus on work.
Simply stated, our talent is no longer focused solely on work
during work hours. Consequently, we must be flexible in how
we define the work day and the workplace.

The meaning of success is being redefined

Fact: Baby boomers, for the most part, really wanted to climb
the corporate ladder as high as they could; such ambition was
seen as a key measure of career as well as personal success.
Later generations are redefining what ambition and success
mean to them. Increasingly, these definitions don't include
trying to climb very far up this ladder … much less all the way
to the top. For example, research external to Deloitte reveals
that 80% of the prime candidates for promotion would like
to work fewer hours than they currently work. This distinction is a major difference from their baby boomer parents. For
example, in 1992, 66% of college-educated men wanted to
move into jobs with more responsibility. In 2002, that number
had dropped to just 50%. Among college-educated women,
this measure of ambition went from 56% to 35% in the same
period. No organization is exempt from these trends.

Implication: Gen Xers and millennials favor family and personal time over the rewards that usually accompany increased
job responsibility. Today's talent is working hard, but they are
often not willing to work harder. They are wary of the perceived costliness of trade-offs they would have to make by
advancing into jobs with more responsibility.

Fact: There is a significant difference between the proportion of baby boomers who are focused totally on work and those millennials and Gen Xers who are work-centric. The survey results shown below also indicate that millennials are far more family-oriented than baby boomers.

Relative Priority Placed on Work Versus Family	Millennials	Gen Xers	Baby Boomers
Work-centric	13%	13%	22%
Dual-centric	37%	35%	37%
Family-centric	50%	52%	41%

Source: *Generation and Gender in the Workplace*, 2002 (see references section)

Implication: About one in seven Gen Xers and millennials describe themselves as work-centric, compared to about one in four baby boomers. It appears that for most people in their early 40s or younger, there is virtually no interest in the traditional approach to career: total focus on work. When dual-centric (evenly divided focus on work and family) and work-centric people are added together, just over half of the working population is willing to place some, but not exclusive, focus on their career.

The reasonable conclusion is that we need to find different ways to engage our talent; we're the ones who will have to be much more flexible in how we conduct business.

All this talk of work–life balance, flexibility, and the like attracts the wrong kind of people to us. Our competitors, who don't emphasize these things, must be getting the ones who are work-centric.

This is wishful thinking. I talk to individuals representing a wide range of organizations and everyone mentions the change in work ethic. In addition, the recognition by Deloitte of the need for balance, flexibility, and new ways to get work done shows progressive thinking and makes Deloitte a very attractive employer.

Reflections on the mega-facts and mega-implications

It's challenging to manage what may not be fully understood or experienced. Our success has always depended on our adaptability and, in the future, will be measured by our ability to develop not only additional flexibility and choice, but also new leaders who understand what today's workers are facing as they manage their personal and professional responsibilities.

A significant change in family patterns has taken place as we've moved from an industrial-based economy — one characterized by centralization, standardization, interchangeability, and hierarchy — to a knowledge-based society characterized by customization, creativity, and networks.

Creativity and imagination in client service require focus and commitment. A knowledge worker's ability to contribute ideas and work imaginatively is reduced if he or she is preoccupied with personal matters. A genuine culture of flexibility and choice creates an environment in which everyone is responsible for the high quality and timeliness of the final product. In such an environment, there is less focus on the specific schedule of when or where the work is accomplished. The benefit to our business is a more nimble and efficient organization with increased capacity to meet client needs effectively.

The flattening of organizational hierarchies due to technology and the need to work with clients who perhaps still operate with a matrix-style structure add another level of complexity to our job. Navigating adeptly through networks will become far more important to business success.

Chapter Six: What's in it for me? from three viewpoints

Ultimately, enlightened self-interest must be served. By decoding the three viewpoints of employer, employee, and team, we uncover an effective way to connect in a mutually beneficial way.

What employers get from hiring millennials

- Community service orientation.

- Technological savvy.

- Flexibility/persistence in the face of change.

- High skill level in social networking activities.

- Strong desire for a long-term relationship with an employer.

> But they ask so many questions. We've got work to do – we don't have time for this.

How else are they going to learn? How did you learn?

Yes, they do ask a lot of questions. But consider it an opportunity to teach these young people how to be professionals.

They really do want to be mentored and coached. They really don't want to make mistakes. As a consequence, they seek continuous feedback, and they will respond positively to it.

The following story illustrates this point[1]: The CEO of a niche software business was meeting with his managers. They, of course, were under constant pressure to produce while under very tight deadlines. During this meeting, his managers were complaining vehemently that they couldn't get any work done because they were constantly being interrupted by young staff members. The CEO listened patiently and then said, "Ladies and gentlemen, you are well paid to be interrupted. How else are they to learn? I don't want to hear about how someone isn't developing and later find out that it was because you weren't answering their questions."

> I hear you. But they ask questions that challenge how we do business ... what could they possibly know given their inexperience?

This is true. But consider a situation in which the millennials' willingness to ask a question about a sacred cow led to the resolution of a problem that benefited everyone.

A group of millennials approached an audit partner complaining about a physical inventory scheduled for the upcoming weekend. "We already have weekend plans and this inventory interferes with those plans," they lamented. "Why can't the inventory be taken during the week? Would you ask the client if this is possible?"

The request did not go over well with the partner. "I'll fix these kids," he thought. "I'll relay this request to the client. 'No change,' will be the answer and that will be that." So, the partner told the story to the client. "I am so glad that you brought this topic up. We're having trouble getting our people to show up for the weekend, so let's move the physical inventory to a weekday," the client replied. What happened next? The partner became a hero to his staff. "We can learn something from these millennials and their willingness to question activities that we take for granted," he concluded. "I learned that it is possible to do business differently and not to be overly concerned about possible client reaction."

Granted, not every situation can have this kind of positive outcome. However, in my experience, the very act of really listening to comments and suggestions, combined with the willingness to be flexible in how we get things done, goes a long way toward winning the commitment and trust of these young people.

Here's another illustration of millennials questioning business fundamentals:

A very talented young tax associate had resigned to take a job in industry after just three years. One of our partners was trying to learn more about the decision that led to the departure of yet another talent from the practice. The tax associate cited the unrelenting deadlines, the extreme difficulty in making definite social plans with others outside of work, the uncertainty that all the hard work would really pay off in more interesting work, etc. The partner's response was typical: "I hear you, but that is the nature of the beast." The young associate replied, "Then maybe you need to find another beast … your current beast isn't going to work out for you much longer." This story accurately depicts the skeptical mindset that is asking fundamental questions about how we conduct our business. It is up to us to either help young workers get comfortable with our current beast, or work together to find another more serviceable beast.

One final comment on this constant questioning … when you find yourself becoming annoyed, remember: These young people have a large gap to close between their experience as technology natives and their skepticism and inexperience relative to the way the traditional work environment operates. How else are they supposed to learn if not by asking questions?

For reasons already discussed they will not accept being told to "just do it." Managers are under no obligation to grant every wish millennials may have, but the savvy manager takes questions seriously and uses them as an opportunity to impart knowledge.

What's in it for millennials as employees

- Working with positive, bright talent.
- Challenge.
- Continuous learning from peers and experienced senior colleagues.
- Working in a collaborative, supportive environment.
- Flexibility.
- Career customization.
- Highly competitive pay over a career.

The aforementioned represent considerable benefits to millennials. In addition, they want to be mentored by senior talent. They want to make an impact on their respective communities and on the environment. We at Deloitte possess these qualities that millennials value highly. We just need to execute more consistently.

What's in it for us working together as a team

- A chance to leverage the best qualities of each generation.

- A chance for young people to learn how to be professionals as well as business leaders.

- A chance for young people to teach others how to use technology more effectively.

- A workplace that uses the full dimension of available talent.

As a team, working in this new, more flexible way gives us a chance to leverage the best qualities of each generation. That means young people can learn how to be professionals at the same time that older or less knowledgeable team members can come up to speed on their technological skills. In a sense, it will be a workplace that uses the full dimension of talent available to it.

Part II: How we decode

So what have we done to adapt to the new realities in the workplace? Plenty. Following are a number of solutions we've initiated. Note that we link each of the solutions discussed with the realities raised in Part I, e.g., three dilemmas, 3 R's, 3 C's, and three divides. It will be clear from this linking that much has been done and much more needs to be accomplished.

These solutions are presented in rough chronological order of implementation, including any pilots.

Chapter Seven: Coaching and Career Connections

Through research and observation,[1] we know that employees of all ages would like a little help when it comes to their careers and what comes next. However, this guidance seems especially needed (and appreciated) at the beginning of a person's career. Our talent wanted to know their options for moves within our many businesses. However, they didn't trust their supervisor to know about available options, nor did they think the supervisor could be objective since a move implied leaving their supervisor's team … and the probability in their minds of a burned bridge.

This hypothesis was corroborated in post-departure surveys conducted by an independent third party. The paper-based surveys were returned by mail. To elicit further details, telephone follow-up surveys were conducted for a representative sample. Individuals were surveyed at least six weeks after leaving Deloitte. We discovered that about two-thirds of the exiting talent went to another employer to do something they could have done with us. However, they believed that changing jobs within Deloitte was too risky or painful to be a viable option.

So, in October 2002, we created a Web-based virtual coaching and career guidance program entitled Coaching and Career

Connections (CCC). Our virtual coaches have provided one-on-one or group coaching to about 10,000 Deloitte employees. More than 40,000 individuals have accessed the CCC Web site (an average of 2,500 to 3,000 hits per week). The Web site is a career planning resource that can be utilized with or without a virtual coach. We believe it has had a direct impact on our keeping between 800 and 1,000 individuals. Their retention equates to savings of between $120 and $150 million. In addition, CCC has helped to facilitate a culture of internal mobility that we know will increase the retention rate of our high performers.

> So we're providing a shoulder to cry on at my expense ... how sweet. What do we really get out of this?

Plenty. We have the retention savings mentioned above. In addition, CCC has engendered a culture of confidential inquiry about careers and internal mobility. The value to Deloitte (or any employer, for that matter) of actively and effectively meeting a key expectation of talent is, as they say, priceless.

Primary realities addressed:
- Experienced talent dilemma.
- 3 R's and 3 C's, especially respected, coached, connected.
- Attitudes toward big business divide.

Chapter Eight:
Team Effectiveness and
Management (TEAM) process

The TEAM[1] mission is to foster effective, innovative, and flexible ways of working to better manage workload and client, team, and personal commitments. This powerful, action-oriented tool engages the entire team in a structured internal process to:

- Zero in on causes of excessive workload, inefficiencies, frustration, and work-life conflicts.

- Develop practical, innovative, and sustainable solutions that are within the team's control.

- Establish "quick wins" that have an immediate impact on team communication, morale, and effectiveness.

TEAM was created in response to a need that grew out of the impact of 9/11 on the Deloitte practices in New York City and environs. Our talent was scattered far and wide as a result of heavy damage to our offices at the World Financial Center. We needed to be able to both conduct business as usual and to communicate with one another … even if it was done virtually.

With that in mind, we created the TEAM process in conjunction with an outside consulting firm, WFD Consulting. The key features of TEAM include:

- An online automated TEAM Assessment Tool to facilitate the process.

- Online reports with aggregate team results to focus discussion, problem solving, and action planning.

- An ability to track issues and time spent on low-value work across teams and functions.

The online automated TEAM Tracking System:

- Captures and documents key issues, outcomes, and action plans.

- Tracks team progress relative to action plans and measures results and business impacts.

- Enables tracking of issues, trends, work innovations, best practices, and business impacts across teams and functions.

> *Sounds like a nice thing to do, like flossing my teeth regularly ... but is it really necessary? Besides, who has the time to devote to the upfront work necessary?*

This comment reminds me of an individual who couldn't attend a much-needed time management seminar because she couldn't figure out how to fit it into her schedule. To improve any process requires realization that a break with the past must occur and that leadership of the project must show the way by investing upfront time in planning. Our experience is that such an investment in TEAM provides more than commensurate returns as the project progresses. The necessary ingredient to realizing the benefits of this methodology is consistent leadership from the top of the project team.

Primary realities addressed:
- 3 R's and 3 C's, especially respected, coached.
- Technology and attitude toward big business divides.

Chapter Nine:
Personal Pursuits:
time off for personal goals

We introduced the Personal Pursuits program in 2005[1] in a continuing effort to respond to our talent's desire for more flexibility and choice in their personal and professional lives. This program allows participants to take up to five years off to pursue personal goals with the expectation that they will remain "plugged in" and return to work at Deloitte. In other words, it provides on-ramps and off-ramps for young talent who need to cycle more readily between personal and professional intervals in their careers.

What's special about this program is that it:

- Further enhances our ability to recruit and retain highly talented professionals as well as deepen their commitment to Deloitte.

- Keeps participants technically competent, tied to our culture, and prepared to re-enter our workforce.

- Addresses the reasons most frequently cited for not returning after an extended break — dormant professional networks and feelings of being technically "rusty" — by helping individuals maintain their professional networks through an assigned mentor and continuing access to CCC.

- Contains learning sites on our Intranet.

> Sounds like another "nice to have" ... but what does it cost and how do you measure effectiveness? All this seems "squishy" to me.

Personal Pursuits is another example of a strategic business tool that helps us customize careers. There is no real cost to this program. If you're concerned about real cost, take a look at what it costs to bring in experienced talent from a shrinking external talent pool in terms of recruiting infrastructure, search fees, on-boarding, related ramping up time ... and the list goes on. So it's a no-brainer to have such a program that can keep us connected to talent we already know can do the job while making it attractive to return to us.

Primary realities addressed:
- Readiness and experienced talent dilemmas.
- 3 R's and 3 C's, especially respected, coached, connected.
- Attitudes toward big business and consumer mindset divides.

Chapter Ten:
Talent Market Series

To keep our eyes — and those of potential employees — focused on the 3 dilemmas, 3 R's, 3 C's, and 3 divides, we've produced a series of straightforward and informal executive briefings on people-related topics called the Talent Market Series (TMS).[1]

The target audience is Deloitte's partners/principles/directors, but we encourage further distribution both within and outside Deloitte. Our focus is a quick, productive read — no more than 3,000 words per volume — designed to provide useful nuggets of information on every page.

The initial volumes, in order of issuance, are:

- *Connecting Across the Generations in the Workplace* — what business leaders need to know to benefit from generational differences.

- *Flexibility and Choice* — what business leaders need to know to connect across the generations in the workplace.

- *Catching the Coaching Wave* — what business leaders need to know about coaching in the workplace.

- *The Deloitte Pre-College Outreach Program* — what

business leaders need to know about broadening and deepening our talent pool.

> *If you haven't noticed, there is a lot of "essential" reading material to choose from. So what makes you think we're reading this stuff, or if anyone has read it, that TMS had any impact worth noting?*

One of the clearest indications of impact is that we've been challenged to keep the volumes in stock, especially volumes one and two. Further, we know that these first two volumes have been used on campus and in client meetings. Finally (and most satisfyingly), our fellow partners/principals/directors have reported that they've taken these volumes home to get family input and were told that the TMS material is on point.

Primary realities addressed:
- 3 R's and 3C's, especially consulted, connected.
- Attitudes toward big business divide.

Chapter Eleven: Pre-College Outreach Program

We'll spend a bit more time on this program because it has implications for Deloitte's businesses, and especially big businesses.[1]

What's on the horizon?

Fact: Opinions about colleges and careers are formed in middle and high school. Young people have reservations about working for big business because of what they see as an overemphasis on profit. Remember, they want to work for the "good company," one that has a more balanced focus between people and profits.

Implication: Teens are thinking seriously about careers based on limited knowledge. We can influence the direction of their thinking, but we need to start at the middle-school level, and possibly as early as 5th grade.

Young people expect interested employers to reach out to them through branding activities … and in ways that let them know who the employer is and what the employer does. The basic attitude is, "We pay attention to businesses that pay attention to us, those we know."

So, before we can interest young people in what we do, we have the added challenge of overcoming their negative perceptions about big business.

Fact: The talent shortfall is real.

As we discussed in Chapter One, the research on the current U.S. high-school population provides a glimpse into just how tight the labor market could become if we don't start creating more interest in careers related to our business.

Implication: Competition in the talent marketplace will be even more fierce than it is today.

What should we conclude from this?

Simply that we need to expand the pool from which we recruit talent. It requires increasing young people's interest in business and showing them our value to society at large. To that end Deloitte has initiated the Pre-College Outreach Program consisting of:

1. LIFE, Inc.
2. Virtual Team Challenge for High School.
3. Business Smarts.
4. Future Leaders Panel.

In focus groups, young people told us that they'd like career guidance and would look very favorably on an organization that helps them. So, we plan on being there for them. Our goals are to:

1. Differentiate Deloitte with a suite of Next Generation tools under the Pre-College Outreach Program umbrella.

2. Expand the future talent pool by creating positive awareness at a critical time in a young person's career decision-making process.

3. Brand Deloitte as a highly desirable employer who helps young people make critical career decisions.

L/FE, Inc.

Our goal is to help young people, especially middle- and high-school students, answer one of life's biggest questions with more confidence: "What am I going to do when I grow up?"

This program provides them with tools that will inform and inspire, and builds an optimistic outlook on their futures. To help us accomplish this goal, we have teamed up with Neale Godfrey, a best-selling author of books on how to educate children about money. She has written 16 books dealing with money, life skills, and values. Her book *Money Doesn't Grow On Trees: A Parent's Guide To Raising Financially Responsible Children* hit No. 1 on *The New York Times* best-seller list.

Her newest book, *LIFE, Inc.: The Ultimate Career Guide for Young People,* gives tips and tools to help young people formulate visions about future possibilities in an interactive way. It also offers interviews with virtual role models — some are our own professionals — who look back on their careers and share insight into their own personal decision-making process.

In addition, an accompanying Web site encourages young people to look at their likes/dislikes and talents in innovative and interactive ways. The fact that we're communicating their way by using gaming techniques and assessments tools makes this program especially appealing to young people.

Along with access to the Web site, school and after-school programs will receive:

1. The Teacher's Guide: Lessons (can vary between 5 and 10 depending on the time available).
2. The Student Journal: A personal journal for self-discovery.

Virtual Team Challenge for High School

Deloitte's Virtual Team Challenge for High School (VTCHS), an online business simulation, engages young people with games, music, and the Internet to help them understand and appreciate the value of what we do as professionals. The simulation is conducted in classrooms twice a year over a four-week period. In the current version of VTCHS teams of four students, working as their own virtual event production companies, compete online against other teams in their class, their school, and across the nation. The objective is to stage a festival that raises the most virtual money for the United Way's current "Operation Graduation" campaign, which encourages young people to stay in school.

At the beginning of each weekly session, teachers introduce one of four content themes that are featured and reinforced in the simulation that week:

- Business.
- Ethics.
- Money.
- Decision-making.

VTCHS is a direct, branded way into tomorrow's talent

pipeline. The simulation requires students to demonstrate our shared values and understand our relationship with the broader community. This experience helps us identify future talent and positions us as the standard of excellence in the minds of students during critically formative years.

The teams that raise the most virtual money are presented with award certificates at regional ceremonies co-hosted by United Way. The competition is a way for United Way to encourage young people to get involved with organized charities such as its own. Deloitte will make a contribution to the winning high schools.

Business Smarts

Deloitte's Business Smarts program began in 2002. It introduces high-school students to the complexities of business. It also helps them discover how they can use their talents, interests, and skills to become a part of the business. Business Smarts is a teacher-directed curriculum with student activity sheets that allow young people to experience careers in professional services. A comic book-based version of Business Smarts for middle-school students, called *Open for Business*, was introduced in 2005 and focuses on entrepreneurial skills.

Future Leaders Panel (aka the Deloitte Insiders)

In 2005, we piloted a Future Leaders Council with six high-school students and six college students from across the country. The council met twice a year to advise our senior leadership on how attractive we were as a career choice and if our strategies for talent acquisition and management were on target.

We concluded that while this was a great idea, it was too limited in scope and impact. Accordingly, our plans are to create a panel — a virtual online council — called the Deloitte Insiders. The Insiders will be young people ranging from fourth graders to college seniors (generally aged 9 to 22) with whom we will consult on a regular basis via surveys. We'll also conduct periodic virtual "town hall" meetings attended by our senior leadership team. Insiders will be selected from nominations made by the talent of Deloitte.

Our talent will be asked to submit candidates, who can be their children, grandchildren, nieces, nephews, neighbors, friends, etc. In addition to the surveys and virtual town meetings, members will have access to a Web site that allows them to learn about career opportunities at Deloitte and to explore the LIFE, Inc. Web site. With its games and other cool features, we hope it will be a Web site that young people will return to on a regular basis.

> All this seems a pretty elaborate way to simply interest kids in what we do. It seems a waste. Won't these kids change their minds about their careers anyway?

Young people expect branding from employers who are interested in them. The programs described here may seem expensive, but the cost is not nearly as great as the cost of our failure to have enough talent to meet client demand.

Because of the time needed to get specific academic training for credentialing purposes, we have little choice but to connect with young talent when they're making major career decisions.

> *Who has time to devote to these programs? This all seems unrealistic.*

All of these programs except the Future Leaders Panel are teacher-led classroom activities. This approach permits our people the flexibility needed to vary the extent of their involvement.

> *What color is the sky on the planet where you live? How do teachers have time to do these activities? Kids can barely read and write these days as it is without their time being redirected to nonacademic subjects.*

The response from educators on planet earth has been very enthusiastic. Teachers know what needs are not being met by current curricula. To their credit, teachers are finding the time to deliver these programs, which fill significant gaps in their students' knowledge and experience.

A parting thought about this initiative

We're largely in new, uncharted territory. This outreach program is a big start. However, if the supply predictions are anywhere close to being correct, we will be challenged to make up the deficit. Thus, we are studying ways to supplement the lack of qualified people by bringing back into the workforce seasoned professionals who can help us train young people and fill important positions that require experience.

Primary realities addressed:
- Readiness and experienced talent dilemmas.
- All three divides, especially attitudes toward big business.

Chapter Twelve:
Mass Career Customization (MCC)

Formal flexible work arrangements (FWAs) are not the ultimate answer when confronting a workforce that is clamoring for more flexibility. FWAs were designed to increase adaptability of the workplace to a changing workforce. However, through our research and observation[1] there is mounting evidence that FWAs, as they are typically implemented, have not delivered on their full potential. The reason is that, as administered, FWAs have shortcomings that can limit their effectiveness in three ways: reach, scope, and concept.

In terms of reach, if FWAs are single programs or if they have to be negotiated on a case-by-case basis between an individual and his or her supervisor, they can be too narrow. Too often the impact of the FWA on the rest of the work team and the customer/client is not given equal weight as the decisions are made. In addition, the case-by-case nature of these arrangements makes them difficult to scale up to the entire workforce.

FWAs can be limited in scope because they address only one dimension of a person's career — schedule, ie, hours worked per day or days worked per week — but do little to address changing needs over the course of an employee's career.

Finally, and most importantly, they can be limited in concept — especially if they are positioned as accommodations (and therefore compromises) to the traditional ideal of full-time employees who will do anything to climb the corporate ladder, rather than as a strategic business tool to help achieve the adaptable or flexible workplace.

As we've seen already, the employees who soon will make up a majority of the workforce have very different notions of what they want out of work. They may appear to be slackers to those who hold to a traditional view of the workplace (though studies show they work as many hours and as hard as more experienced workers); however, in reality this emerging workforce is just not willing to make the traditional trade-offs, which they perceive as sacrificing too much of their family and personal lives. They insist on both meaningful work *and* meaningful personal lives.

Women, who already comprise 50% of the workforce and 60% of students in American colleges and universities, have long been striving for this shift in priorities, and now men are just as likely to feel this way as women. As a consequence, organizations must find ways to build adaptable work cultures that are rewarding to both women and men of current generations — and inviting to future ones.

> *Wait a minute ... at Deloitte we've had a formal FWA program for years, to say nothing of informal flexibility we encourage. Are you saying none of this has had a positive impact? Have we been wasting our time – are we throwing out FWAs?*

Not at all. Formal FWAs are a logical place to start when an organization has little or no history of fostering an adaptable or flexible workplace. So that's where we started at Deloitte. By studying our undoubted successes with FWAs — and some failures too — we realized that even if formal FWAs were better administered they could never have the reach we'd require if we were to realize our strategic ambition of building a flexible workplace attractive to the emerging workforce. Furthermore, the encouraging of informal flexibility was simply too vague and unfocused to have the desired impact.

> *So you're saying formal FWAs and other traditional forms of flexibility may be OK places to start, but they can't take us to the "house"? I'm all anticipation ... please produce the magic bullet.*

The magic bullet is ... cue the drumroll! ... customization. Our research shows that workers want the ability to make reasonable choices about fitting their lives into their work and their work into their lives ... not just on a limited basis, but over the course of their careers.

MCC: A better approach

Borrowing from the trend toward mass customization in consumer products, we've crafted a program for mass career customization that fills the gap between the traditional one-size-fits-all and custom-made approaches.

MCC moves away from rigidly administered flexibility programs to a more cohesive model by which employees can adapt important career dimensions to their individual needs. It is built on the following principles:

- The retention of key talent depends on cultivating a sense of loyalty and connection.
- Flexibility and adaptability over time are critical to both individuals and organizations.
- Transparency regarding trade-offs and choices leads to better decisions and greater satisfaction.

The practical effect of implementing MCC is to:

- Recognize that careers ebb and flow over time and provide a more fluid structure in response.
- Institutionalize a consistent framework/process.
- Enable well-considered choices.
- Make trade-offs more explicit.
- Provide greater transparency.
- Extend the boundaries and consistency of what's acceptable.

Business as usual is not an option

- Today's career path is no longer a straight climb up the

corporate ladder but rather an undulating journey of climbs, lateral moves, and planned descents.

- FWAs in the way they are usually administrated are a reasonable starting point, but they are limited in the scope of problems they can effectively address and in scalability.

- Rather than climbing the corporate ladder, knowledge-based workers will scale a "corporate lattice™," allowing them to climb upward via paths that are more fluid and adaptive.

Our MCC program provides a wide range of options for creating careers that suit employees' needs today while also addressing future circumstances and priorities. Individual choices are likely to involve the four major dimensions of career: role, pace, location/schedule, and workload. While the options available are not limitless, they do allow employees to calibrate each of the four dimensions that define their work experience based on their current aspirations and life circumstances.

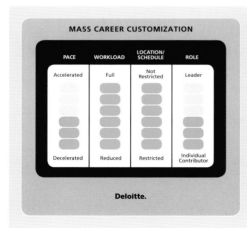

Career Dimensions

Pace: Options relating to the rate of career progression

Workload: Choices relating to the quantity of work output

Location/Schedule: Options for when and where work is performed

Role: Choices in position and responsibilities

Source: *Mass Career Customization* (see references section)

MCC resolves the "my life doesn't fit into my work and my work doesn't fit into my life" conundrum for the employee — while allowing the employer to retain top people, reduce turnover, and build a strong talent pipeline.

For example, someone who chooses to reduce his or her workload by 50% will likely trade off advancing through the organization at the same pace as someone with a full workload. Similarly, someone who chooses to telecommute five days a week may need to accept the trade-off that he or she can no longer stay in a role that requires face-to-face meetings. As these examples suggest, a key component of MCC is articulating the trade-offs in a way that is clear and consistent, but also adaptable to individual situations.

A success story (one of many)

Tina, an audit partner, was hired 11 years ago into a staff position. She worked full-time and progressed at an average rate early in her career, advancing to senior staff three years later. Tina was then able to accelerate her career and earn an early promotion to manager by continuing to work full-time at an exemplary level of performance. Within her first year as a manager, Tina took a three-month maternity leave with her first child. She returned to her position at a 90% workload and continued at this level for the next three years.

While on maternity leave with her second child, Tina was promoted to senior manager at a pace that was standard within the practice at the time. She returned as a senior manager at a

70% workload. She subsequently demonstrated strong performance, and as a consequence, her pace to partner was accelerated. She was accepted into the partnership after three years as a senior manager while working a 70% schedule.

Since becoming a partner, Tina has been working an 85% workload and telecommuting one day a week. While her workload is less than full-time, she adjusts her schedule to the cycles of work and home, working full-time during the busy audit season and fewer hours during the summer when her children are home and work demand is lower.

MCC unifies individual types of flexibility into a cohesive and consistent system.

> Right ... but we've got a business to run. MCC seems difficult to pull off ... tightening up administration and using a particular FWA when it makes sense for all concerned should be sufficient.

MCC is a solution that's a natural step in the development of an organization that has both the ambition and ability to become, and remain, a premier employer of talent. FWAs and informal forms of flexibility, when properly handled, will benefit any organization. Therefore, there is no real business reason for an organization not to adopt these traditional policies and practices. However, these basics have now become "table stakes" … the expected minimum to get into the game as a viable employer for talent. To reemphasize, our ambitions and abilities compel us to "kick it up a notch" — we believe MCC is that necessary next step that will permit us to keep our place among the most sought after employers of talent.

A final thought on MCC

MCC requires the rethinking of every aspect of the employer/ employee relationship. Managers will have to be more coach, less boss. Employees will have to be more active in directing their own careers and more accountable for results. Leaders will need to be consistently visible sponsors and role models for this new paradigm and the organization will need to align every aspect of human resources management — from performance and compensation review to the way training is delivered. The measures of success will be the stability of key talent pools, the strength of the leadership pipeline, and the depth of employee engagement and connection. For us, it's already working.

Primary realities addressed:
- Experienced talent dilemma.
- 3 R's and 3 C's, especially respected, coached, consulted, connected.
- Attitudes toward big business and consumer mindset divides.